ticktock

CONTENTS

Words that appear **in bold** are explained in the glossary.

Copyright © **ticktock Entertainment Ltd** 2008
First published in Great Britain in 2008 by **ticktock Media Ltd**,
Unit 2, Orchard Business Centre, North Farm Road,
Tunbridge Wells, Kent, TN2 3XF
ISBN 978 1 84696 777 1 pbk
Printed in China

We would like to thank Penny Worms, the National Literacy Trust, and our consultant Downs Matthews, Director Emeritus, Polar Bears International

Picture credits
t=top, b=bottom, c=centre, l-left, r=right
Alamy: OFC, 6-7, 8-9, 10-11, 13, 14-15, 16-17, 18t, 19, 20, 22-23, 25, 27t, 28b.
Corbis: 4-5, 12, 18b, 21, 27b, 29b, 31, 32.
Every effort has been made to trace the copyright holders, and we apologise in advance for any unintentional omissions. We would be pleased to insert the appropriate acknowledgements in any subsequent edition of this publication.

LIFE IN THE ARCTIC

The Arctic is the **habitat** of the world's biggest land **predator** – the polar bear.

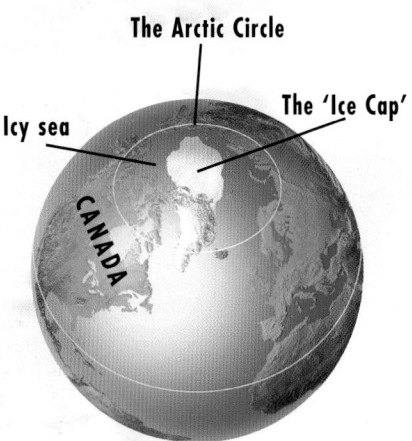

The Arctic Circle

The 'Ice Cap'

Icy sea

CANADA

In the Arctic Circle a large area of the sea is frozen all the year round. This is called the 'Ice Cap'. In winter, the sea around the Ice Cap freezes, too.

Polar bears spend the autumn, winter and spring hunting on the frozen sea.

MOTHERS AND CUBS

In early winter, a female polar bear will build a den by digging into a snow bank. Her cubs will be born here, two metres under the surface.

The mother bear will make a narrow air hole into the den and the family will live here right through the winter.

BABY FOOD FACT

In the den the cubs will feed on their mother's milk. The mother only has her body fat to live on.

LEAVING THE DEN

In early April the family will leave the den.

The mother has had nothing to eat for months, and she must hunt for food. If she doesn't eat, her family will not survive.

Hungry predators, such as wolves and adult male polar bears, will be on the look-out for bear cubs to eat. The mother must guard the cubs carefully.

Polar bear families stay close to the den for the first two weeks.

A LIFE IN THE SEA

Polar bears are strong swimmers. They spend a lot of time in the sea swimming from **ice floe** *to ice floe, hunting for seals.*

They have webbed feet which they use as paddles. Their thick, oily fur keeps them warm in the freezing water.

Polar bear cubs quickly learn to swim. If they become tired, they can travel through the water on their mother's backs.

FINDING FOOD

The polar bear's main food is seals.

Bears wait at holes in the ice. When a seal comes up to breathe, the polar bear will pounce and kill the seal with a blow from its paw.

Polar bears spend over half of their time hunting. They may catch a seal once every four to five days.

HELPING THE NEIGHBOURS

Adult polar bears mainly eat seal **blubber**. They leave the meat. This is eaten by young bears and other animals such as Arctic foxes.

HUNTING POLAR BEARS

*The **Inuit people** of northern Canada have always hunted polar bears for their meat and fur.*

When hunters from other parts of the world started to come to the Arctic to hunt polar bears for sport, too many bears were killed. Laws were passed to limit the hunting.

Now only a few bears can be hunted each year by the Inuit people, and all hunters need a licence.

A NEW DANGER

*Now there is a new danger for polar bears – **global warming**.*

Polar bears need the floating ice to hunt seals. Global warming is causing the sea ice to melt earlier and freeze later. If there is no ice in the spring and autumn, polar bears have less time to hunt.

The ice-free sea also makes it difficult for polar bears to travel. Bear cubs and young bears cannot swim the long distances between the ice floes.

COMING TO TOWN

Sometimes hungry polar bears will come into the towns of northern Canada looking for food.

Polar bears will not usually kill humans unless they are angry or frightened, but they are dangerous. People in the towns need to be protected.

Special hunters shoot the polar bears with a dart gun to send them to sleep. The polar bears can then be taken to a safe place by helicopter.

This bear is searching for food on a rubbish dump.

STUDYING THE BEARS

Scientists also use dart guns to find out about polar bears so they can help them.

Scientists can weigh a sleeping polar bear. If finding food is getting more difficult, polar bears may be getting thinner. Regular weighing helps to keep a check on this.

KEEPING TRACK

Sometimes polar bears are fitted with radio collars. These collars are used by scientists to track the polar bears and see where they go to hunt.

A DIFFICULT FUTURE?

It is thought that there are 25,000 to 40,000 polar bears in the Arctic. Life may be very difficult for them in the future.

Global warming is damaging their habitat and making it hard for them to hunt.

Mining and drilling for oil are causing **pollution** and changing the **environment** where they live.

A lot is being done to save polar bears. Scientists now know a lot more about them, and fewer people are hunting them.

Polar bears can survive into the future – but they will need our help.

In this picture scientists are studying polar bears from a special bus. Some of the people are on a bear-watching holiday.

GLOSSARY

blubber A layer of fat around the body of animals such as seals, whales and polar bears.

environment The area where an animal or plant lives, and all the things, such as weather, that affect that place.

global warming The heating up of the Earth. It is caused by gases in the air trapping in heat from the Sun.

habitat The place that suits a particular wild animal or plant.

ice floe A floating sheet of ice.

Inuit people Native Americans who have lived in the Arctic for hundreds of years. They fish and hunt for seals and polar bears.

pollution Oils, rubbish or chemicals that have escaped into the sea or air, or onto the land.

predator An animal that lives by hunting and eating other animals.

INDEX